STUDY GUIDE

Galatians

The Gospel of Abraham, The Law of Moses

Galatians Study Guide

The Gospel of Abraham, The Law of Moses

Authentic
LIFESTYLE

First published in 2003 by Authentic Lifestyle

09 08 07 06 05 04 03 7 6 5 4 3 2 1

Authentic Lifestyle is an imprint of Authentic Media,
P.O. Box 300, Carlisle, Cumbria, CA3 0QS, UK
and P.O. Box 1047, Waynesboro, GA 30830-2047, USA

www.paternoster-publishing.com

British Library Cataloguing in Publication Data
A catalogue record for this book is available from the British Library

ISBN 1-85078-505-8

Cover Design by Diane Bainbridge
Typeset by WestKey Ltd, Falmouth, Cornwall
Printed in Great Britain by Bell & Bain Ltd, Glasgow

Contents

For Richard Bewes, Rico Tice and Paul Williams, for such generous fellowship in our ministry together

Study 1, Galatians Chapter 1

Paul, an Apostle of God's Gospel

Key Truth: Paul writes this letter to explain how trusting in Christ gives us true freedom.

1. The Letter of Freedom

The very first thing that should strike a visitor to a Christian church is the freedom which is experienced there: freedom from social boundaries, economic expectations, peer pressure, traditional lifestyle, class consciousness, political agendas; freedom from pretence and slavish conformity. Onlookers should see and recognise that here at last is a people who live with dignity. Here is a people of true FREEDOM. Galatians is the book that not only gives us such a vision, but shows us how it can be a reality in all our own lives.

If we go anywhere else in society, we get dragged along by other peoples' agendas, campaigns, promotions or ideas. We are drawn into compromise and complacency. But in the Christian Church we find a group of people who are part of something different, a people who see that the world doesn't move according to the trivial and empty assumptions of the age. The Church, when she is true to herself, is the one place where we can look reality in the eye and understand where the centre of gravity lies. The Church is the place of liberation from all false power, the place where real power is understood, the power and authority of the Living God of the Bible. The Father, Son and Holy Spirit are the answer to all problems and they are the way that people from all different cultures and backgrounds can unite.

Everything else promises us what it cannot deliver. We are told that sexism lies in the past, yet it dominates the world around us in new and depressing ways. We are told that our careers will satisfy us, yet we are reduced to commodities and live for nothing but the weekend. So few of us ever do what we dreamed. We are helplessly controlled by the pop-culture or the counter-culture, or we are too lost to even know that we are controlled. We know that reality is more than flesh and bone, but how can we ever access it? The religious rituals, the meditation, the dietary regimes, the new philosophies, the life management programmes, the expanded consciousness and the ancient traditions ... all these are built on nothing more than flesh and bone. Where is the spiritual reality that is beyond these all too human efforts?

Paul in his letter to the Galatians shows us that the answer is to be found in Jesus, the Messiah promised and hoped for since the beginning of the world. There is freedom in Him. All fleshly categories that constrain people are blown apart by His life, death and resurrection. When we come to the Messiah we find the answer to all things. He is the hope and desire of the ages and the nations. The Messiah gives us the answer rather than a list of new questions. He is the definition of the Church, not any ethnic or religious boundaries.

2. The Attack Against Paul and the Gospel

If, today, we had gone to the Corinthian church of Paul's day we would have been shocked and appalled by their behaviour, with their sexual immorality, drunkenness and arguments. However, if we'd have walked into the Galatian church, we would have seen everyone behaving well. We'd have seen lots of respect for the Scriptures and a zealous religious lifestyle. We might perhaps think they were slightly legalistic, but on the whole we would probably feel challenged by their commitment. But of all the churches Paul deals with, he never gets so upset as he does here at the Galatian church. Why, when it seems a respectable moral church?

Paul's letter to the Galatians addresses the ultimate spiritual challenge. For 1500 years the Living God prophesied the life, character, work, death and resurrection of the Messiah through a system called The Law. It was given through the great prophet Moses at Mount Sinai, the mountain of God. John 1:45 tells us that Moses was writing about one Person, the Messiah, in his record of the Law. This system was the ultimate signpost to the coming Messiah, describing every feature of the righteousness of the Father, Son and Holy Spirit. When the Messiah – God the Son – came, the Law had served its purpose and came to an end.

The book of Galatians addresses an evil teaching introduced into the young congregation by false teachers who trusted in the Law of Moses rather than in the Messiah prophesied in the Law of Moses. They clearly wanted to undermine the apostle Paul in the minds of the Galatians, which is why Paul has to lay his life open in this letter. The heart of their attack on Paul is that he was depending on his own human arguments.

They had accused him of undermining the Scriptures and the Law of God. They argued that the Scriptures actually teach that people join the family of God by trusting in the Law.

In human terms, the false apostles had plenty to criticise Paul for. He used to persecute the Church (1:13) and he was the last apostle to be chosen. But Paul, along with every other Christian, is not subject to human judgement. He makes the point over and over again in these opening chapters that he was appointed by Jesus, who instructed him personally; and by God the Father, who raised Jesus from the dead. He shows that his calling by Christ was a) ordained since birth (verse 15), b) by God's grace alone since he had previously persecuted the Church intensely (verses 13 & 14), and c) all he needed for apostolic ministry. Paul did not consult other Apostles before he had authority to teach himself. Paul did not care what the world thought about him. He had not been appointed by mere men, nor even taught by men.

Paul boldly defends himself in this chapter and the next because if he is discredited, then so is the Gospel he has been preaching. It is important that they understand who he is and what his authority is. He doesn't do this so that the Galatians will give him glory, but so that they may know he speaks the very words of God.

Paul explains his movements in detail after his conversion in verses 17–22, expanding the brief outline of his movements in Acts 9. He does this to prove that his teaching is not passed on from other men, it comes directly from Jesus. He was obviously not part of the well known Jerusalem set because the churches of Judea knew hardly anything about him (verses 21&22). In fact, the only report those Christians had heard about him were of his amazing transformation by God. The Judean churches had every reason to suspect Paul, verse 23, and believe that his teaching was false. They must have been extra critical because they knew that he had previously persecuted Christians. However, when the Judean Christians heard him, they recognised that he was not preaching an earthly message, but the true gospel from the LORD – verse 24. How much more, then, should the Galatians have trusted him since they knew him well.

3. The Gospel and the Law

The issue in Galatia seemed to be connected to the heresy described in Acts 15:1 – "unless you are circumcised according to the custom of Moses you cannot be saved." These wicked teachers had put forward the idea that a person can only be part of God's family by obeying the Law.

Paul confronts this poisonous message by analysing what is really at stake.

What if we insisted that anybody who wanted to know the Father should put their trust in the Law rather than the Messiah?
What if we took that Law of God and used it as a religious system without trusting in the Messiah?
What if we sinful human beings tried to fulfil all that this Law described?

When Paul answered this unbelievable danger, he set down the bounds of freedom for the Church forever. If even the Law of God cannot replace the Messiah of God, then all other options are ruled out. If the very words of God cannot be turned into a religious system, then all religious systems are shown to be tyrannies and prisons. If the best possible "religious system" is no alternative to the Messiah, then all the lesser, merely human religious systems are shown to be utter rubbish. This is how this letter sets us free from every lie and controlling system.

The gospel of faith in the Messiah is what God has always taught from the very beginning.

Paul shows that the Law teaches faith in the Messiah, not faith in the Law. It is not the Law vs. the Gospel. It is the Gospel & the Law together vs. the world, the flesh and the devil.

4. The Relevance of Galatians

Paul was so angry not just because the Galatian false teachers had misunderstood the Hebrew Scriptures and the real purpose of the Law. Rather in doing that, they were missing the reality of Jesus the Messiah. The truth of the Messiah is not just another system for obeying God, or even THE system for obeying God. They had missed what it is to be a member of the true Israel, the Church, a son of God in the Christ.

The book of Galatians is not like an old 16th Century debate or a technical discussion of Old Testament interpretations. It is a gospel manifesto. We are encouraged to study the Old Testament because it is teaching us the gospel: it's for freedom that Christ has set us free, 5:1.

In the book of Galatians, the apostle Paul will tear any blinkers from our eyes and force us to see what is really at stake in all this. The moment we turn to our own resources, the moment we think we can fulfil the righteousness of the Law of God through our own religious effort (no matter how well-intentioned), we have forsaken Jesus the Messiah completely. The moment we think we can conquer our sins by gritting our teeth and trying harder we have rejected the Messiah. We are members of righteous Israel by faith in the Messiah, not by our obedience to the Law of God.

In verses 3–5 Paul takes us back to the basic truth that our salvation has been given to us by the sheer grace of God in Christ, and is not conditional upon our fulfilment of the Law.

This is the apostle Paul at his most emotional, his most angry. Here he gets to grips with the most fundamental issues in life. Nothing so stirs him; nothing so provokes his deepest convictions as the issues of this book. Here the very essence of the gospel that has underwritten every action of God since the creation of the world is grasped and applied. In no other book is Paul forced to reach so deeply into the very heart of the truth of Jesus the Messiah.

It is interesting to note that in verses 6–9 Paul saves his criticism and scorn for those teaching the false Gospel, rather than those who are believing it. All he says about them is that he is astonished (verse 6). It is a much worse thing to be teaching a false Gospel, (Greek lit. 'a different gospel, which isn't one'). Teachers will be judged more strictly (James 3:1). If anyone should preach anything other than the one and only true Gospel then they deserve eternal condemnation. By saying this in verse 9 Paul is showing that everyone including himself, all men and even heavenly creatures are subordinate to the gospel. The gospel reigns supreme over all creatures. We could actually tell angels to be silent if they are not preaching the gospel!

Paul shows that by the gospel he is teaching he is not trying to win the approval of mere human beings. In fact, all it has earned him is the hatred of both Jews and Gentiles. One cannot be a true servant of Christ and pursue the affection of everybody else as well (verse 10).

In Galatians the agenda is the freedom of the Christian – freedom from legalism and freedom from sin. Paul is the champion of freedom. In the whole history of the world, he is the writer that has refused every kind of tyranny, every imprisonment that degrades the human person, every lie that hides the terrible truth of our condition from us. Any other writer on freedom tends to miss the big picture, the holistic and profound freedom that the great apostle insisted upon. Paul was disgusted that the gospel of freedom, which the absolutely FREE God had achieved for us in Jesus, should be turned into a form of slavery through religion, racism and human tradition.

Galatians will take us to the centre of the Bible and show us what it is all about: the freedom and forgiveness of the family of God in Jesus the Messiah.

Further Questions ...

1. What had the Galatians accused Paul of?

2. Paul describes how the gospel was revealed to him in verse 12. Has the gospel always been revealed in this way down through the ages?

3. If Paul had been set apart to the LORD from birth, verse 15, why wasn't he saved as a child? Why wait until he had killed so many Christians?

Daily Readings ...

Day 1:	Galatians chapter 1
Day 2:	Acts 9:1–31
Day 3:	Deuteronomy chapter 6
Day 4:	1 Corinthians 10:23–11:1
Day 5:	1 Timothy chapter 1
Day 6:	John 17:6–26
Day 7:	1 Corinthians chapter 11

AD	
10?	Born and educated at Tarsus.
37–40	Paul's meeting with Jesus on the road to Damascus, followed by three years personal training from Jesus in the desert. Galatians 1:17.
45–48	**Paul's first missionary journey**. Antioch, Seleucia, Salamis, Paphos, Perga, Pisidian Antioch, Iconium, Lystra, Derbe, and Attalia. Acts 13:13–14:28
49	Council of Jerusalem – Acts 15.
50–52	1 & 2 Thessalonians
50–53	**Paul's second missionary journey**. Jerusalem, Antioch, Derbe, Lystra, Troas, Neapolis, Philippi, Amphipolis, Apollonia, Thessalonica, Berea, Athens, Corinth, Cenchreae, Ephesus, and Caesarea. Acts 15–18:22.
55–57	Galatians
54–58	**Paul's third missionary journey**. Antioch, Ephesus, Thessalonica, Corinth, Philippi, Troas, Assos, Mitylene, Miletus, Tyre, Caesarea, and Jerusalem. Acts 18–21.
57	1 & 2 Corinthians
57–58	Romans
58–60	Paul in prison in Judea
60–61	Journey to Rome
61–63	In prison in Rome
62–63	Ephesians, Philippians, Colossians, Philemon
63–67	Other journeys. He may well have made it to Spain, as he wanted – Romans 1:10, 15:24, 28; 16:1–5. In Clement's first letter to the Corinthians he seems to indicate that Paul accomplished this desire. "After preaching both in the east and west, he gained the illustrious reputation due to his faith, having taught righteousness to the whole world, and **come to the extreme limit of the west**, and suffered martyrdom under the prefects".
64–65	Titus; 1 Timothy; (Hebrews – Paul is a possible writer)
66–67	2 Timothy

Bible Study 1

Chapter 1:6–12

Paul had heard that the Galatians were being taught to put their trust in the Law of Moses itself in order to be saved, and not in Christ, the One to whom the Law had always pointed. He writes to them to put them right.

Why is Paul so passionate about this issue?

What is the difference between Paul's attitude towards the Galatians themselves, and those who have taught them this false gospel? Who bears the responsibility?

Verse 8 is a very powerful statement. Can this help us be sure of our faith in the face of so many other 'spiritualities' today? How can it help when we consider how many cults and other religions often begin?

How can we be equipped to be able to be on our guard against false teachings?

In verse 10, what are the differences between serving Christ and serving men? Why can we never do both these things at once? (See also Matthew 6:24)

When is it most difficult to serve Christ over and above serving people? What do we find most helpful in these situations and how can we encourage each other to do this?

Have we received the gospel in the same way as Paul did? (See Jude verse 3) Why is it important where the gospel comes from and how it is revealed?

Study 2, Galatians Chapter 2

Peter, an Apostle to the Jews

Key Truth: Paul sets forth his argument against trusting in the Law itself for salvation: the Law taught that salvation would come from the Messiah alone.

1. Paul's Visit to Jerusalem, verses 1–10

In chapter 1:18 we learned that Paul spent two weeks with Peter sharing all that he had been taught by Jesus in his desert theological training. He also met with the leader of the Jerusalem church, James, who was a brother of Jesus, born of Mary by the usual means. There was no problem with Paul's message at that time, and he was free to get on with the task of taking the gospel of the Messiah to the Gentiles.

Fourteen years later Paul went back to Jerusalem with Barnabas and Titus – 2:1. The Holy Spirit had told Paul to make this visit, verse 2, presumably to make sure that there was not even the appearance of division between the apostles. Trouble-makers had been trying to undermine the freedom that the Church enjoyed now that the Law of Moses no longer controlled their life – verses 4–5. They had be to opposed or else the temporary nature of the Law would be confused with the permanent reality of the Messiah. Paul made sure that he talked to the Jerusalem leaders privately so that all his work for gospel unity was not undermined by public arguments.

If there had been any doubt about Gentiles being included within Israel, then Titus would have had to be circumcised. However, the leaders were happy to accept Titus as a fellow member of Israel, the Church of God, simply on the grounds of his faith in the Messiah.

The trouble-makers seemed to have been trying to control Paul, verse 6, but he refused to let them add their confusion about the Law to the simple gospel message. Paul kept his eye on God's own judgement rather than the foolish thinking of the Law-worshippers.

The outcome of the meeting at Jerusalem was that everybody could see that Paul had the God-appointed task of bringing the Gentiles into the Israel of God by the gospel, whereas James, Peter and John had the God-appointed task of bringing the Jews into the Israel of God by the gospel – verses 7–9.

However, whether to Jews or Gentiles, they shared the task of caring for the poor within the Church – verse 10. This is no small matter. The sharing of resources between the Jewish and Gentile congregations throughout the world is one of the most important practical signs of the gospel in the New Testament – see especially Romans 15:22–29.

2. Peter's Visit to Antioch, verses 11–13

Things were not so harmonious, however, when Peter made a visit to Antioch.

At first everything was fine. Peter behaved completely in line with the gospel. The great apostle Peter, knowing that the Law of Moses had served its purpose in training the people of God to wait for the Messiah, ate with **Gentile** followers of the Messiah without the constraints of the Law of Moses. Peter had learned a hard lesson in the importance of eating with Gentiles when the LORD Jesus had given him a vision telling him to eat all kinds of meat, including what the Law called unclean meat (Acts 10). Peter knew that eating all food with thankfulness with every person who followed the Messiah, regardless of the obsolete regulations of the Law, was the teaching of Scripture and the truth of the gospel. So, (verse 12) Peter ate with the Gentiles at Antioch, with the apostle Paul. The unity in truth that had been enjoyed in Jerusalem still governed Peter's lifestyle.

Nevertheless, Peter backed down from his confidence in the Messiah when a group arrived from James at Jerusalem.

What had happened at Jerusalem since Paul's visit? Clearly, the trouble-makers had continued to stir up false teaching and unbelief against the Messiah and His people. They probably questioned the freedom that the followers of the Messiah enjoyed. They must have constantly argued for the Law as a permanent feature of the life of the Church, the Israel of God. Because they trusted in the Law rather than the Messiah, they must have hated the way that those who followed Jesus, the real children of Abraham, discarded the Law as merely a temporary stage in the Church's history.

So, 'the circumcision group' seemed to have gained such an ominous reputation in the Jerusalem church that even Peter was intimidated by them. When they arrived in Antioch he began to modify his behaviour so as not to provoke the kind of arguments and opposition that 'the circumcision group' had caused in Jerusalem. Peter actually began to behave as if the Law of Moses were still governing the Church, just as if Jesus the Messiah had never been born! This is why Paul described him as "clearly in the wrong" (verse 11).

Peter's bad example, his practical denial of Jesus, caused other Jewish Christians to lose faith in Jesus (verse 13).

3. Paul Opposed Peter, verses 14–21

Thank God for the apostle Paul. The truth of the Scriptures, the teaching of Moses and the nature of the Law were being fundamentally undermined by the evil influence of 'the circumcision group'. They were intent on turning the Scriptures upside down in order to make the Messiah a servant of the Law! Thank God that the Holy Spirit appointed Paul as the defender of Scripture and the gospel of Jesus. Paul was not about to let these false teachers enslave the Israel of God with their poisonous practices.

Paul's argument to Peter must have been one of the most dramatic moments in the history of the world. These two apostles, foundation stones of the whole Church since Pentecost (see Ephesians 2:19–20), stood face to face over the freedom of God's family. This proves that Paul had no interest in pleasing mere human beings. He feared the Father, Son and Holy Spirit ... and therefore feared nothing else, not even when he seemed to stand alone for the truth of the Messiah.

His argument to Peter is summarised for us in verses 14–21, and it is one of the most powerful arguments in the whole of the Bible.

In verse 14 he simply points to the inconsistency in Peter's behaviour. Jesus the Messiah had set Peter free to be a Jew who could live like a Gentile. If a Jewish Christian had such freedom from the Law of Moses, why didn't the Gentile Christians have such freedom, when they had never been under the Law at any time?

In verses 15–16 Paul makes a devastating point, arguing from the Hebrew Scriptures to a fellow Jew. He seems to cut himself and Peter off from the Gentiles in verse 15, as if he were having an in-house discussion about the teaching of the Scriptures. However, when he explains what the Jewish Scriptures were teaching, we see that Paul will not allow barriers between Jewish and Gentile Christians.

In verse 16, then, he explains that the Jewish student of Scripture knows that (lit.) 'no flesh' will be justified out of works of the Law. This is almost a direct quotation from Psalm 143:2. In this Psalm, David knew that he had no righteousness of his own by which he could stand before God. He was trusting in the LORD not the Law for righteousness. David, in many Psalms, showed that he did not trust in the Law for his acceptance before God.

Paul in verse 17 continues his commentary on Psalm 143. When we draw near to Christ, we see our own sinfulness and the need to rely on Him. But if this is the case, does that mean that Christ brings us into sin? Instead of making us pretend to be holy, Christ shows us that we are sinful. Isn't that compromising with sin? Or, put another way, if coming to Christ means confessing that we've broken the Law, then is Christ all for Law-breaking?

Paul's answer to this kind of thinking is that confessing sin is not breaking the Law – it's keeping the Law! The Law was never intended to be a way for Israel to establish its own righteousness. Paul is showing us that real Law-breaking is trying to establish righteousness by keeping the Law instead of trusting in Christ. To trust in the Law is to abuse the Law.

In verse 18, Paul is reminding Peter that as Jews they have already trusted in the Messiah and therefore they have died to the Law – they had destroyed the Law, seeing it as an obsolete preparation for Jesus. The fact that Peter was now turning back to it proves that he is actually opposing the true purpose of the Law. To turn away from the Christ to the Law is a betrayal of the Law, the ultimate Law-breaking.

This is because the Law's job was only ever to point to Christ. It was there to make the Jews die to the Law and live to God. This he explains in verses 19–21. The Law pointed away from itself and to the Messiah. Peter could either trust in the Law or in the Messiah, who is the One who gives Israel righteousness.

In verses 20–21 Paul sets out the choice between Law breaking and Law fulfilling. As Paul looked to the Messiah, he found himself joined to Him in death. The Law told him that if he was crucified with Christ then he was cursed, (Deuteronomy 21:22–23). However, the LORD told him that if he was crucified with Him, Paul is saved! He cannot be joined to Christ and also trust in the Law. To choose Christ is to fall under the curse of the Law. However, to choose Christ is to die to Law and therefore to escape its curse.

For us today, we can now look at the Law and see what it taught the people of God. If we trust in Jesus, we are doing what the Law requires.

Further Questions ...

1. In the light of Peter's experiences in Acts 10:9–48, why are his actions in this chapter surprising?

2. How, as verse 19, does someone die to the Law and live for God?

3. How is trusting in the Law itself for salvation actually breaking it (verse 18)? In what way should the Galatians have been keeping the Law?

Daily Readings ...

Day 1:	Galatians chapter 2
Day 2:	Psalm 143
Day 3:	Acts 10:9–48
Day 4:	Romans chapter 14
Day 5:	Deuteronomy 21:22–23 & Acts 7:54–8:3
Day 6:	Romans 6:1–14
Day 7:	Acts 11:1–18

Bible Study 2

Chapter 2:11–21

Paul's argument to Peter in these verses helps us to understand that the Law's purpose was always to point Jews to the coming Messiah, Jesus.

Who do you think 'the circumcision group' was and what were they doing?

From verses 11–13, what were the dangers of what Peter was doing?

Peter had been freed from the constraints of the Law because he trusted in the Promised Messiah. Therefore, verse 14, he could live a life of freedom. Why then was it such a bad thing for him to force Gentiles to keep the Law? (See also Acts 10:45–48)

What is Paul's view of the Law in verses 15&16? Look also at David's view in Psalm 143:1–2, which is directly quoted here by Paul.

In what ways does seeking to be justified by Christ cause us to see our own sin? What does this then propel us to do? How is this an explanation of what the Law's job was?

If we understand that the Law's purpose was always to bring people to faith in the Messiah, how does this help us understand why Paul opposed Peter when he turned back to faith in the Law itself?

What does the Law say about Christ's death? (Deuteronomy 21:23) According to verse 20, why couldn't the Galatians choose to trust both in the Law and in Christ at the same time? What must they choose and why?

As united believers in the international gospel of Jesus Christ today, what is our relationship to the Law?

Study 3, Chapter 3:1-25

Abraham, the Man of Faith

Key Truth: Paul takes us back to Abraham to understand the eternal gospel and how the temporary period of the Law pointed to faith in the same gospel.

1. Foolish Galatians, verses 1-5

All that Paul has said so far is laying the foundation for this rebuke – "O foolish Galatians – do you have no understanding?! Are you under some kind of magic spell?!" Paul has recorded so much personal history in order to make it very clear how stupid the Galatians seem to be. They are going against the entire work and struggle of the apostles, not to mention the teaching of the Scriptures and the purpose of the Law.

Jesus was clearly presented as crucified. This is a crucial point, as we see in verse 13. The Law described a crucified man as cursed by God – Deuteronomy 21:23. It was not possible for the Galatians to hold onto **both** a crucified Messiah and the righteousness of the Law. The two realities were in head-on collision.

So, Paul takes them back to the beginning of their Christian life. Did they begin by achieving righteousness through the Law or by freely receiving the gift of the Spirit by faith in Jesus the Messiah? Did they join the Israel of God through carrying out the Law or by trusting in the Messiah of Israel?

What about their ongoing Christian life? Had they moved on beyond the fellowship and power of the Holy Spirit? Is their human effort in fulfilling the Law greater than the power of God the Spirit?

The Christian life is not just about beginning by faith but living by faith every single hour of every single day. We never graduate beyond trusting completely in Jesus and the power of His Spirit. Our Christian existence is trusting Jesus from beginning to end. Carrying out the Law of God as if that was the key to spiritual growth or serious discipleship is a fundamental denial of Jesus.

2. Consider Abraham, verses 6–9

Paul loves to go back to Abraham to demonstrate the truth of the gospel of Jesus. Abraham is **the** foundation figure of the Hebrew Scriptures. He is the father of Israel, the spiritual ancestor of the Church of every age. Whatever is true of him must be true of us all in every generation.

In Genesis 15:6 Moses clearly records that it was because of Abraham's faith in the LORD that he was judged to be righteous before God. That teaches us the pattern for all his spiritual descendants. Faith in the Seed (see verse 19), the Messiah, is the definition of being in Abraham's family. If we trust in the Promised Seed, the Messiah, just as Abraham did, then we are part of Abraham's family. Everybody who trusts in the LORD like Abraham is a child of Abraham, regardless of their ethnic or cultural or religious background.

The LORD knew that the family of Abraham would ultimately cover the entire globe, so He recorded in the Bible the fact that the gospel of all nations was preached to Abraham so very long ago. The **blessing** promised to Abraham comes to people of every nation who trust in the Messiah promised to Abraham.

3. Cursed Israel, verses 10–14

However, there is an apparent block between these blessings and the nations of the world – and that is none other than the Law that the Galatians were trusting in!

The nation of Israel – the people who are of the works of the Law (verse 10) – was under a curse.[1] This is what the Law itself describes in Deuteronomy 27–28. Paul sends us back to study these chapters with the great summary verse of Deuteronomy 27:26.

When Israel received the Law they were placed under the threat of a curse. If they failed to do what the Law required they would be a cursed nation, driven from the Promised Land into **exile** (Deut. 28:36). To join the nation of Israel under the works of the Law is to join a nation under a curse (verse 10)!

Even back in the days of Habakkuk, the Scriptures made it clear that the threatened curse had in fact fallen on Israel (verse 11). The book of Habakkuk begins with the prophet complaining that as he looks at life in

[1] A more accurate translation is "those of the works of the Law are under a curse".

Israel it is clear that (Habakkuk 1:4) the Law was powerless to produce righteousness. The LORD agrees with him and announces that he was already bringing the Babylonians to take Israel away into exile. The curse threatened in Deuteronomy 28:36 had fallen on Israel. So, (Habakkuk 2:4), and this is the quotation in Galatians 3:11, the only righteous people are those who trust in the LORD. A person who trusts in Israel as defined by the Law is trusting in the very thing that the Law has cursed.

But, one of the false teachers at Galatia might say, "yes, but our following of the Law is the way of faith. We do have faith, as Habakkuk 2:4 says, but our faith is in the Law."

Paul directly rejects such a thought – "The righteous live 'of faith'. The Law is not 'of faith'." The Law is not what we must trust in, rather it is the LORD that we must trust in. This is why Paul quotes Leviticus 18:5.

Leviticus chapters 18–19 describe how the LORD's redeemed people must live differently than the pagan world. However, the great theme is not confidence in human obedience to the Law or the ability of Israel to make itself holy by fulfilling the Law. No, the sentence repeated over 20 times is "I am the LORD (your God)". Leviticus 20:7–8 carries on this mighty rhythm with these vital words – "Consecrate yourselves and be holy, because I am the LORD your God. Keep my decrees and follow them. **I am the LORD, who makes you holy**."

According to the Law itself, the trust of Israel was not to be in the Law but in the LORD, the God who had redeemed them and made them holy.

Jesus teaches this most clearly in His own quotation of Leviticus 18:5 in Luke 10:25–37. An expert in the Law came to Jesus with a very Galatian kind of issue – "what must I **do**, what Law must I perform, if I am to inherit eternal life?" Jesus asks him to explain what the Law requires, and the man answers very well – "Love the LORD your God with all your heart, soul, strength and mind and love your neighbour as yourself." Jesus approves of this summary and quotes Leviticus 18:5 – do this and you will live. Notice that Jesus takes Leviticus 18:5 to mean "Love the LORD your God and your neighbour". Of course, the man did not really trust in the LORD for his justification, and (Luke 10:29), "he wanted to justify himself".[2]

The Law itself required that the people of the Law trust in the LORD God for salvation. The Law did not require Israel to trust in the Law for salvation.

So, Israel was under a curse, a curse which only the Messiah Himself could take away (verse 13). The blessings of Abraham could never flood

[2] Therefore Jesus showed him that he was a half-dead sinner who desperately needed mercy, just like the man who received mercy from the good Samaritan.

out to the whole world as long as Israel was cursed under the Law. Part of the work of Jesus Christ was to take that curse on Himself, by dying the cursed death of hanging on a tree. After dying His cursed death, Jesus the Messiah begins His new life in the Resurrection, a life beyond the Law with all its curses. The Messiah is the life of Israel and has taken the life of Israel beyond the Law with its confining and limiting restrictions – (verse 14). Israel under the Messiah is set free to be what was promised to Abraham, a blessing for all the nations, a global community made up of Jews and Gentiles.

4. An Everyday Example, verses 15–18

Paul takes the example of a will that is signed and sealed – verse 15. A will is not an ongoing process of negotiation nor is it open-ended. The will is a final statement. It is a completed and final arrangement.

Therefore, Paul takes us back to the time when the original terms of the LORD's "will" were set out. He investigates the original form of the covenant that has governed the relationship between the Living God and His people for all ages. In doing this Paul is reaching back in history to the time before the Law of Moses was ever given by God. Paul's basic question is this: what is the foundational covenant that the Law of Moses fits into?

Here Paul shows what a careful Bible student he is. He turns to the promises (not laws) given to Abraham at the very beginning. Paul doesn't just skim over the words. He zooms in to see that the promises were not given to lots of individual Israelites on the condition that they fulfil the Law of God. No, the promises referred to just one individual Person – the Messiah (verse 16).[3] It is the Messiah (and the people united to Him) who stands in the blessings of Abraham.

Now, if the original covenant is a promise referring to the Messiah and the proper response to that from Abraham was faith, trust in the Messiah, then how can the Law be something different to that? How can the Law be opposed to, or inconsistent with, the original gospel to Abraham? Of course it cannot be (verse 17).

When the Law was given through Moses, it did not over-rule or change the original promise to Abraham. It did not say that the righteousness of Israel was to be achieved through works of Law. The Law is completely consistent with the original promise: "Look to the Messiah. The promise is to Him. Righteousness depends on the promise of God in Christ." The

[3] The original will and covenant was a promise from the Most High God to His Messiah, a promise between God the Father and God the Son.

very fact that the covenant was a **promise** shows that it never depended upon Israel fulfilling the Law – verse 18.

5. What was the Purpose of the Law? verses 19–25

So, we might ask, if the original gospel preached to Abraham was 'trust in the Promised Messiah', what was the point in bringing the Law in to confuse things? If the only thing the Law did was to bring a curse upon Israel, then why did the LORD God bring the Law at all? Surely the original promise to Abraham was enough.

Why the Law? (verse 19) Paul's answer is just one word – transgressions (Greek lit: Sin.)

While Israel was waiting for the Messiah, the Seed to Whom the promise referred, there was the constant problem of sin. In the long wait, Israel in its sinfulness constantly strayed off and began to trust in other gods for its righteousness. The Law came to confront the sin of Israel and daily point forward in all of life, constantly, to the Messiah in Whom their righteousness was to be found. The Law covered every aspect of life, from food to clothes, from animals to business, from social relationships to agricultural practices, from skin diseases to building construction. It covered so much of life so that every day from dawn till dusk Israel could live a life focussed on the coming Messiah. The purpose of the Law was to confront sin and unbelief, while pointing firmly to the Promised Seed.

In verses 19–20 Paul treats us to one of those brilliant bits of Bible study that remind us how carefully we need to read the Bible. It was always clear that the Law was not replacing the promise to Abraham **because of the way it was given at Mount Sinai**.

The promise referred to 'one' (Greek: henos), verse 16, who is Christ. In verses 19–20 Paul returns to this idea of 'one' (Greek: henos).

Here is a literal translation of the Greek in these verses: "Why then the Law? For sins it was added, until the Seed came to whom the promise was made. The Law was administered through angels by the hand of a Mediator. The Mediator is not one (Greek: henos). God is one (Greek: heis)."

The Law was given by the **hand** of the Mediator[4], which seems to refer to Deuteronomy 9:10 where we are told that the Law was written by the finger of God.[5] Paul reminds us that when the Mediator gave the Law, He

[4] The NIV misses out the Greek for 'the hand'.

[5] In Exodus 19 and Exodus 33-34, we learn that it is the second Person of the Trinity who was the Mediator, mediating the Unseen LORD in the giving of

was not alone (Greek: henos), but was accompanied with a host of angels.[6] The Promise referred to **one**, not **many**. It referred to the Messiah alone, not a whole host of angels, therefore the Law could not be the fulfilment of the Promise.

God is one (Greek: heis). This might be a reference to Deuteronomy 6:4, which explains the different word used for 'one' here. When the Living God fulfils His promises, He does so personally and alone. In His promise He swore **by Himself** – Genesis 22:15–18. The LORD promised **Himself** as Abraham's very great reward – Genesis 15:1.

The gospel promise concerns the Living God alone, and there are no assistants or agents in His work of salvation. The Promise is what God does **alone**; the Law was what angels do for Him. The Promise of the Messiah is internal to God; the Law was external to God, administered by angels. The gospel is what God is doing Himself – the Father sending the Son, the Messiah. The Law was what the Son, the Mediator, administered through angels.

So what WAS the purpose of the Law?

Verse 21. If the Law was not what the promise referred to, was the Law actually against the promise? If the Law was a cursing, temporary arrangement administered by angels rather than the LORD Himself, then is it harmful to the original promise?

Certainly not! The Law was not the fulfilment of the original promise, but the Law was completely on the side of the Promise. The Law was on the side of the promised righteousness. In fact, the Law was so committed to that righteousness that if it was possible for it to come by the Law it would have done. However, righteousness could never come by the Law because of human sinfulness. The Law could only point to the promised righteousness of the Messiah, showing up the sinfulness of the human heart and the desperate need for the Messiah.

---

5 (continued) the Law. There is a Person called the LORD who can be seen (see Exodus 24:9-11), even seen face to face (see Exodus 33:11). This Person is the divine 'Angel of the LORD' who travels with Israel (see Exodus 3:1-6; 13:21-22; and 14:19-20). This LORD introduces another Person called the LORD who is hidden in thick darkness, whose face cannot be seen (see Exodus 33:21-23).

6 Deuteronomy 33:1-2 makes this clear – "This is the blessing that Moses the man of God pronounced on the Israelites before his death. He said: 'The LORD came from Sinai and dawned over them from Seir; He shone forth from Mount Paran. He came with myriads of holy ones from the south, from His mountain slopes.'" Hebrews 2:2-4 also tells us that the Law was spoken and enforced by angels.

In verse 23 Paul re-emphasises the argument of verse 19 – the Law was given to watch over the Church because of its sinfulness. This Law was a kind of tutor so that the people of God would have the truth of the Messiah drummed in, in spite of their sin and unbelief. On first reading verses 23–25 it sounds almost as if there was no faith before the birth of the Messiah, but this would be going against all that Paul has just argued about Abraham's faith! We must remember that by 'the faith' here, Paul is not saying that before the birth of Jesus people were not saved by faith – because in 3:6–9 and 3:6–14, Paul has specifically argued that the message of Abraham, Moses and the prophets was 'have faith in the promised Seed'. By 'the faith', he is referring to the One promised, the One in whom the believers of every age trusted. We could put it like this: now that object of the faith of Abraham and Moses has come, the supervision of the Law is no longer given.

This chapter is deep and stretching. The apostle has made us dig deep into the Scriptures to uncover the true nature of the Law and the Promise of the Messiah. We might be wondering why we needed to do so much work. However, to understand the Old Testament and the Law, to understand that 'trusting in the Messiah' has only ever been God's one way of salvation is of profound importance. Not only will this show us how to read the Old Testament, but we will be able to resist all false teaching and corrupting thinking that leads us to put our trust in anything or anyone other than Jesus the Messiah.

Further Questions ...

1. How did Christ's death on the cross put an end to the Law?

2. Why did God decide to have the period of the Law at all, if it was only ever faith in Christ that mattered?

Daily Readings ...

Day 1:	Galatians chapter 3
Day 2:	Genesis chapter 15
Day 3:	Romans chapter 4
Day 4:	Leviticus 18:1–5 & Habakkuk 2:2–5
Day 5:	Genesis 12:1–9 & Revelation 7:9–17
Day 6:	Hebrews chapter 11
Day 7:	Luke 10:25–37 & Matthew 5:17–20

Bible Study 3

Chapter 3:6–9 & verse 14

Paul is arguing to convince the Galatians that the Law itself never could bring salvation. This was always through the promise of the gospel message, as demonstrated for us by Abraham.

Verses 6–9 tell us about Abraham's faith in the gospel. Look at Genesis 15:4–6. Who was it who appeared to Abram and spoke with him here? (Remember that John 1:18 tell us that no one has seen the Father at any time).

Who did Abram trust in? (John 8:56, Hebrews 11:8–10)

How does Abram's face-to-face encounter with one of the Persons of the Trinity encourage us to look on him as a model of the Christian faith, even today?

What does it mean when we are called children of Abraham? (See also Romans 9:6–8)

Look at verse 8. In what way is this quotation from Genesis 12 the message of the gospel for the whole world? What is being referred to? (See Matthew 1:1 & 17)

During the period of the Law, was it possible for Gentiles to be saved at all? If so, how? (Look at Exodus 12:48–49)

According to 3:14, what is the difference in the way the Gentiles are saved after Christ's death put an end to the period of the Law?

What have we learnt about the Law from this chapter? Do we need to worry about keeping its rules and regulations today? (3:24–25)

What have we learnt about the gospel? Has it changed since Abraham's day? (Hebrews 11:11–13 and Hebrews 13:8)

Study 4, Galatians 3:26–4:31

Sarah, Mother of the Free

Key Truth: The signpost of the Law no longer restricts the Church. By serving this, the false teachers were encouraging slavery to that which was set in place to serve. In the Spirit, through faith in Christ, we are children and heirs to gospel freedom.

1. The Law as a Guardian, verses 26–29

The Church must not live under the Law because the time of the Law is over now. To allow the Law to control us would indicate that we did not understand that the Messiah has already come.

The time of the supervision of the Law over the Church is over. Israel has burst out of the limits of the Law. The temporary school of the Law has been closed and the Church has reached its age of maturity. Jesus the Messiah has taken Israel out of the laborious instruction of the Law into His freedom and responsibility. Whether originally Jew or Gentile, all Abraham's seed are outside the Law's tutorials.

The Law drew a line around Israel, marking it off geographically, socially, ethnically from the rest of the world. The Law controlled the life of the Church before the Messiah's arrival, separating men from women, Jew from Gentile, slave from free (verse 28).[1] There were laws to control all these aspects of life. The Messiah has ended the function of the Law and through baptism we are identified as living with Him in the global promises given to Abraham (verse 27).

---

[1] The Law in all its aspects no longer defines the life of Israel. The food laws, the menstrual laws and the economic laws, which all bore witness to the Messiah, are no longer binding the Church. They are all obsolete in the global Israel.

2. A Family of Freedom, verses 1–7

A child is under supervision while careful instruction is given in the ways of adult life (4:1). At that time the child seems to be just like a lowly slave – and certainly the angst-filled teenager tends to feel that! However, they are simply being prepared for all the freedoms, opportunities and responsibilities of adult life (4:2). This time is forward looking. When the child matures and stands face to face with their former teacher as an adult, the purpose of the time of restriction and instruction is clear (if they had a good teacher!).

So, the life of the church needs to be seen over the long span of history, from Abraham through to today (4:3–4). In Abraham, the Church was reminded of the gospel of faith in the Messiah, with promised blessings for the whole world. From the time of Moses, because of sin, the Church entered a temporary time of restriction and instruction when the responsibilities and freedoms of the family of God were learned. This time actually restricted the international ministry of Israel, but only so that a time would come when Israel could span the whole world much more effectively.

Now that the Promised Messiah has come, the time of instruction is finished. Now the Church is welcomed into the family of God as an adult, ready to enjoy the freedoms and bear the responsibilities of the full life of Israel across the whole globe (verse 5). So, the Holy Spirit welcomes us as adult members of the divine household, crying out in our hearts that we are sons and not slaves (verse 6). As sons we are the heirs of the household, waiting to receive the family heirloom, which is the entire creation renewed in Jesus the Messiah at His glorious appearing – see Romans 8:15–25.

3. Demonic Slavery, verses 8–20

Now, if the glorious Church of God endured a time of slavery, this is infinitely more true of the Gentiles who had never known the promises of Abraham and the righteous instruction of the Law (verse 8). The Galatians, as Gentiles, did not know the Living God of Israel at all before they trusted in Jesus. They were slaves, not to the **useful** teaching of the Law, but to the foul and depraving ways of "those who by nature are not gods" – that is, mere demons or idols (see Deuteronomy 32:16–17, Isaiah 37:18–20).

It is **not** that they managed to find out about the Holy One of Israel through their own religion or philosophy. Rather, the Father, Son and Holy Spirit graciously found out about them through the powerful gospel (verse 9)! Their escape from slavery was not through obedience to the Law.

Having been set free from the pathetic slavery of pagan unbelief, why go back into slavery? (verses 9–11). Surely, having escaped slavery they should be fanatics for freedom! The only ones wanting them to trust in the Law rather than the Messiah are the evil demons who had misled them in the first place.

1 Timothy 4:1–5 tells us that the demons try to deceive us into trusting in legalistic practices, because they want to deny us our maturity and freedom in Christ. Instead of trying to get us to behave in outrageous excess (as in films and novels), a demon may well be trying to get us to trust in obeying the Law of God instead of Jesus.

The Galatians were listening to these 'weak and miserable' **Stoicheia**, verse 9, a word that seems to describe some of the angels and spirits who rule over humanity – see also Colossians 2:8 and 2:16–23. We hear about these ruling powers throughout the Bible – see Ephesians 6:12. They are under the ultimate command of Satan himself (Ephesians 2:2). The **Stoicheia** seem to be a variety of evil demons who use the obsolete Law of God as a way of enslaving humanity, drawing us away from Christ to childish restrictions.

Instead of understanding how everything in the Law was a shadow of Jesus the Prophesied Messiah, the Galatians were continuing to keep all the Sabbaths, festivals and seasons of the Law as if they were an end in themselves! Instead of learning the lessons of those festivals and walking in the liberty of Christ, they were simply continuing to enact the shadows, **trusting in the signpost rather than the destination**. There is demonic power behind such foolishness.

4. Paul's Anguish, verses 11–20

If that is really where the Galatians are at spiritually, then Paul needs to begin with them as complete unbelievers, totally ignorant of the gospel, verse 11.

Paul takes them back to the time when he arrived to share the gospel with them (verses 12–15). He wants them to remember their spiritual birth when they first trusted in the Messiah. At that time they were so thrilled with their freedom in Jesus that they treated Paul like a angel from God, verse 14. Even though Paul was struggling with what seems to have been a bad eye disease (see verse 15), yet they loved him dearly with great joy.

Paul (verses 19–20) is in pain and perplexity about the Galatians because he cares for them so much. He is so desperately keen for them to be free in the Messiah that he feels as if he is in childbirth, giving all his energy and emotion to their spiritual birth. Paul will know that they are safe in the spiritual maternity ward when they are zealous for the freedom and maturity of Christ. The false teachers are the opposite (verses 16–17). They are selfish, not giving of themselves for the Galatians, but expecting the Galatians to become their disciples. They are not overjoyed by the gospel, but trying to alienate the Galatians from their gospel parent, the apostle Paul.

5. Hagar and Sarah, verses 21-31

Paul challenges the Galatians, to see how serious they really are about the Law. If they are such careful students of the writings of Moses, then surely they understand all that Moses was teaching? Paul loves to show that Moses was teaching exactly the same gospel message – see Acts 26.22–23.

Matthew Henry, the early 18th Century Bible scholar says this: "In these verses the apostle illustrates the difference between believers who rested in Christ only and those judaizers who trusted in the law, by a comparison taken from the story of Isaac and Ishmael."

Paul goes back to the life of Abraham, but this time focuses on Sarah and Hagar. Paul treats us and the Galatians as very serious Bible students in these verses. Usually Paul patiently helps us to understand the original meaning of the Scriptures, but here he gives us a challenge. He expects us to know the Scriptures as well as he does, so most of us need to work hard to keep up with such a careful Bible scholar!

Abraham had two sons, one through the flesh[2] by a slave woman (Genesis 16:1–4) and the other through the power of the Spirit by a free woman, fulfilling the LORD's promise (Genesis 21:1–5).

Paul then asks us to think more carefully about why the LORD allowed these historical events to happen in this way, and why Moses recorded them for us. When we study the lives of these two women with their children we see that Moses is teaching us about the difference between trusting in the power of the flesh and trusting in the power of the Spirit, trusting in the law of Sinai and trusting in the promised Messiah-Seed.

The lives of Sarah/Isaac and Hagar/Ishmael seem strange mirror images of each other.

- Both received promised blessings from the LORD: Sarah/Isaac in Genesis 18:13–19 and Hagar/Ishmael in Genesis 16:9–16.
- Isaac, through Jacob, produced 12 tribes – Genesis 35:22–29. Ishmael produced 12 tribes – Genesis 25:12–18.
- Both Isaac and Ishmael were true children of Abraham: Isaac by the power of the Spirit and Ishmael by the power of the flesh.

---

[2] The NIV translates the Greek word *sarx* (flesh) as 'in the ordinary way'.

The similarities and contrasts between the two invite us to think carefully about them.

Hagar's life was a life of **slavery**. She was the servant of Sarah, and even when she ran away, pregnant with Ishmael, the Angel of the LORD told her to go back and **submit** to Sarah – Genesis 16:9. The blessings for Ishmael were given only after the command to **submit** to Sarah was given.

Hagar and Ishmael ultimately refused to submit to Sarah and in Genesis 21, after the birth of Isaac, Ishmael's unwillingness to serve Isaac causes Hagar and Ishmael to be driven out of the free family of Abraham into the desert (21:14).[3] Although the Angel of the LORD heard the prayers of Ishmael, yet the slave boy and his mother turned away from the Promised Land and lived in the desert of Paran (Genesis 21:21).[4] The Greek word 'arabia' in Galatians 4:25 simply means 'desert'.[5]

Paul draws all this together in Galatians 4:24–26 in one of the most profound examples of Bible study in the New Testament.

Hagar and Ishmael, the slaves of the free woman, end up in the desert of **Paran** outside the Promised Land. This is no accident. In Deuteronomy 33:2 we see that when the LORD came from Sinai with myriads of angels to administer the Law (see Galatians 3:19) He came from **Paran**. That is the mighty beginning of Moses' great final address to Israel before his death.[6] The first thing Moses wants to say about the Law in this massive closing address is that **the Law was given, through angels, at the place of Hagar and Ishmael**.

Paul challenges us to study the Law more carefully. When we study with his rigour and enthusiasm we see that Hagar, Ishmael, Sinai and the Law all go together. All of them are outside the Land of Promise, all of them are in submission to the promise. They are all servants of the free. The job of all of them is to serve the promise. None of them are the fulfilment of the LORD's gospel promise.

The earthly city of Jerusalem displays this most clearly. Paul, like other Bible writers, takes it for granted that there are **two** Jerusalem's[7] and this may well confuse the English reader. However, the Hebrew word Jerusalem is grammatically a dual, which means it refers to two places. Every time the word is spoken it speaks of two cities!

So, the earthly Jerusalem belonged to the administration of the Law, the way of slavery. It was only ever a signpost pointing to the glorious

[3] Galatians 4:29-31.

[4] See also Genesis 25:18.

[5] See Strongs number 688.

[6] We get the same truth recorded for us in Habakkuk 3:3.

[7] Hebrews 12:22; Revelation 3:12; 21:2, 10. We can see the same thing in Psalm 87, though the word Zion is used there to refer to the heavenly Jerusalem.

heavenly Jerusalem, the City of the Living God. To invest in the earthly Jerusalem rather than the heavenly Jerusalem is to show a complete misunderstanding of how the earthly served the heavenly, the slave served the free.

Paul refers us to Isaiah 54:1 – "Sing O barren woman!". This call to sing comes, of course, after the wonderful description of the work of the Promised Seed, the Suffering Servant (Isaiah 53), who through His sufferings and death would bring forgiveness and blessings to His offspring – the offspring of The Offspring, the seed of The Seed (Isaiah 53:10). The important children are not those of the flesh, but those of the promise.

By faith in the Promised Messiah we are given birth into the **reality** that all the **signs** of the Law pointed towards. We are children of the promise not the flesh. We are citizens of the heavenly Jerusalem not the earthly shadow. We are part of the permanent covenant of Abraham rather than the temporary covenant of Sinai. We are the free not the slaves (Galatians 4:31).

It is the free children born into the gospel reality by faith in the Messiah who inherit the family treasures, 4:7. The slave woman and her son (4:29–32) refused to submit to the free woman and her son so they were driven out, denied any part in the inheritance of the Promised Land.

So, the false teachers who were trying to trap the Galatians have no part in the inheritance in Christ. They admit to putting their confidence in that which only **serves** the gospel **freedom**. If they choose the servant instead of the free, they show that they are children of the slave, children of Abraham only in the flesh, rather than children of the free, children of Abraham according to promise.

The point of Paul's mighty Bible study is to show us that the Scriptures prepared for the service of the Law in advance. The LORD God wanted to show His people how to understand the Law, how to distinguish between the slave and the free. It is vital that we understand this lesson, so that we can live as the free showing the amazing truth of the Messiah to the world. There is such deep confusion about how to live, how to relate to spirits, religious rituals and even food. **The people of the Messiah are the only people in the world who understand true freedom and live within it**.

Further Questions ...

1. Look at 4:4. Why has Paul specifically noted here that Christ is born of a woman, and born under Law? What does that have to do with redeeming us from the Law?

2. The Stoicheia (mentioned in verse 9) are a particular group of angels. Look at other references to them throughout the Bible (Galatians 4:3, 3:19, Ephesians 2:2, 6:12, Colossians 2:8, 2:16–23). What do you think their job was? What do they do now?

3. When reading the account of Sarah casting out Hagar and Ishmael in Genesis 21, we often pity Hagar and think Sarah cruel. How does verse 30 here show us the correct perspective on this story?

Daily Readings ...

Day 1:	Galatians chapter 4
Day 2:	Genesis chapter 16
Day 3:	Genesis 21:1–21
Day 4:	Romans 8:1–27
Day 5:	1 Timothy chapter 4
Day 6:	Isaiah chapter 53
Day 7:	Isaiah chapter 54

Bible Study 4

Chapter 3:26–4:7

The temporary instruction that the Church experienced whilst under the Law has now come to an end. The mature Church now enjoys freedom and unity in Christ through the Spirit.

Verses 26–29. What things bring us to the LORD?

What does it mean in these verses to be in the family of God?

What do these verses mean for the person who has been living by the restrictions of the Law of Moses? How would reading this affect their lifestyle?

In 4:1–3, Paul looks at the history of the Church (the heir) from Abraham to today. What does he mean when he calls the heir "a child" here? Which period of time is he talking about? (Remember Galatians 3:24–25)

How does this illustration help us to understand the Church's time of slavery and instruction under the Law, and freedom in Christ?

How did the death of Jesus change the Law forever? Why is Paul so upset that the Galatians were turning back to follow the Law?

How does the Holy Spirit set us free, and what is His role in our relationship with the Father? (See also Romans 8:26, Exodus 35:30–35, Galatians 5:22–23)

Study 5, Galatians Chapter 5

The Spirit, The LORD of the Free

Key Truth: Our freedom in Christ by the Spirit enables us to love and serve each other and not be enslaved by sin.

1. It is for FREEDOM That Christ has Set us Free, verse 1

In chapter 5, Paul reaches the conclusion of his argument concerning Christian freedom and verse 1 is in many ways a summary verse for the whole letter.

Serving the Law is serving what is itself a servant. That is in effect being a servant to a servant. However, we are the free! – we're not even servants of the free, we are free ourselves, 5:1.[1]

Paul wants us to have a much higher view of the life of the Church. As free Christians, the Galatians should be able to look at the Law and see it for what it is – a servant for just a period in the Church's life. The Church has now entered the time of maturity and freedom.

What Paul wants for the Galatians is that they do not run away to the servant Law when they face food, clothes, animals, business, sex, and so on. We should have a proper understanding of all these things rather than needing a guardian to supervise all the time. Paul wants us to live as responsible adults in the family of God. When we come to think about food we should understand that we can eat anything we want to as we thank the Father for His generous provision (Romans 14:6; 1 Timothy 4:3). When we deal with clothing, we should understand that our beauty or dignity is not based on mere clothing but on our godliness (Matthew 6:25–34; 1 Timothy 2:9; 1 Peter 3:3). When we deal with sex and sexuality, we understand the way Adam & Eve were created in the image of

[1] Angels administered the Law, but we will judge the world and angels (1 Corinthians 6:2-3).

God as equal but different, united in marriage as one flesh (Genesis 2:21–24).

For the sake of the world around us it is vital that we are not enslaved by all the agendas and lies of the world. If we live and think like unbelievers there is no point in us telling everybody that Jesus is the promised Messiah, the Saviour of the world. If we live as unbelieving, immature slaves, then how can we claim to have been set free as children in God's family?

Outside of the church there are no answers to the deep questions of reality. What is the universe? What about the unseen world of angels, spirits and demons? What happens to the dead? Do planets and stars have power over us? What's the meaning of life? How can we understand our sexuality? Etc, etc.

In joining the Church, a person comes into a community which has been instructed in reality for thousands of years. The new believer therefore comes into a mature body of believers who have 100% reality. As a new believer, we might have to do a lot of Bible study in order to be able to 'catch up', to understand where the Church is now. As a unity, a body, we are mature.

The amazing wonder many of us feel when we first become Christians and realise that everything has been done for us and given to us, is often watered down as the pressures of service and of the work of our peers convince us we need to do something to remain in God's favour. In writing Galatians, Paul will have none of this. He simply wants his readers to know beyond a shadow of a doubt that if we belong to Christ, everything required for our salvation and our on-going Christian life is ours, completed and finished.

This freedom must transform our lives. As Martin Luther said: "Who can describe our state when we are assured in our heart that God neither is nor will be angry with us, but will forever be a merciful and loving Father to us for Christ's sake."[2]

Not only have we been set free, but we have been set free for freedom! Not only are Christians set free when they become Christians, but they are set free **for freedom**, to be and to remain free!

Paul saw the hideous influence that was creeping into the Galatian churches. The false teachers would say that Christ sets the Gentiles free from their pagan lives, BUT the Gentiles are free to obey the Law like a Jew. They might have said "you must obey the Law to keep you free from Gentile lifestyles". Paul says "No!" Christian freedom is **real** freedom – it

---

[2] Luther's commentary on Galatians. Crossways Classic Commentary edition. Page 241.

is not freedom to be a slave! It is not freedom to simply carry out instructions.

The whole issue of freedom is of course a topic that constantly needs the Biblical perspective. The unbelieving world will tell us that real freedom is the ability and power to do anything, whether good or bad, moral or immoral, right or wrong, helpful or harmful. The Living God, in the Bible, teaches us that some things enslave us rather than free us. To choose to do what enslaves and depraves is not an act of freedom.

2. Circumcision and The Law, verses 2–6

Is Paul being anti-Semitic here in his criticism of circumcision? Of course not. In other places he states clearly that there is much value in being a Jew and in circumcision (Romans 3:1–2). He even circumcises Timothy in Acts 16:1–3. Here however, the context is Gentiles becoming full members of Israel, as followers of Jesus Christ. Do they have to be circumcised in order to be 'grafted into Israel'?[3] In that context, circumcision means nothing at best, but at worst it can become (as it did in Galatia) a bondage leading people to be enslaved away from Jesus.

Circumcision on its own is of course not the major issue. In verse 3 Paul highlights the real problem. Circumcision is part of the Law and if the people in the churches in Galatia decide that the way to retain God's favour is by observing the Law, they have missed the whole point. By trusting in even one aspect of the legal observance, they will be demonstrating that they have not understood or accepted what it means to trust in Jesus.

The false teachers began with circumcision as the first constraint on Christian freedom. Paul sees through their evil intentions and tells the believers that the Law comes as a whole (verse 3). You can't pick and chose those bits you are going to obey and those you aren't. You either observe the whole Law and thus demonstrate your lack of trust in Christ, or you observe none of the Law and completely trust the words and works of Christ.[4]

John Chrysostom commenting on these verses says: "He that is circumcised is circumcised because he fears the Law, and he who fears

---

[3] See Romans 11:13-24.

[4] Wesley says the following:

> For in Christ Jesus... neither circumcision (with the most punctual observance of the law) nor uncircumcision (with the most exact heathen morality) achieves anything towards present justification or eternal salvation. But faith alone – even that faith which works by love.

From Wesley's notes on Galatians.

the Law, distrusts the power of grace, and he who distrusts can receive no benefit from that which is distrusted."[5]

Paul concludes this verse by anticipating the question that has arisen since he began this letter. If the Law is not necessary for Christian living, what is necessary? The only thing that counts is faith expressing itself through love.

3. Running a Good Race, verses 7–12

Paul is both deeply concerned for the believers in these churches and deeply angered by those who are teaching them such falsities, verses 7 & 10. He reminds them again (as he did in chapter 1) of how they began their Christian walk.

Instead of the original truth about the Messiah, they have become corrupted with a totally false human message that is like a computer virus working its way through the entire system and doing enormous damage as it goes. To put faith in the Law rather than the Messiah is the gravest abuse of the Law of God and will bring a heavy penalty (verse 10).

Paul's faithfulness to the true gospel has brought him plenty of trouble (verse 11). The 'circumcision group' persecuted him because he unmasks their trust in the Law for the sinful rebellion that it was. Those who were teaching the need for additional measures to ensure Christian security weren't being persecuted. Their message was easier to swallow. Religion is always more acceptable than trusting Jesus.

Few of us are so upset by false teaching as the great apostle Paul. Few of us love the Church so much that any harm against us causes such grief. Paul reacts strongly to any attack on the precious Bride of Christ, the Church of the firstborn, the Israel of God. The false teachers, who were abusing the Galatian church which he had planted, attract Paul's harshest words.

Perhaps the closest analogy might be that of a loving parent reacting to the person who has abused their beloved child. That would make any loving parent furious with rage. That is the feeling the apostle expresses in this verse. Let's pray that we would all react with such horror when we hear teachers and people in positions of authority in the church, teaching falsehood and leading Christ's followers away from Him and into slavery.

[5] Chrysostom's commentary on Galatians 5:1.

4. Using our Freedom, verses 13-15

Paul addresses the inevitable question – 'if we are so completely free, can we just sin if we want to? If we have such total freedom, then why don't we just use our freedom to be sinful?'

To even ask such a question, though, is the mark of slavery and not freedom. It is like a person asking why they can't use their health in order to become sick. Paul warns us not to abuse our freedom by being slaves of our sinful flesh (verse 13). Instead of seeing our freedom as a tool for selfish, sinful desires, we need to understand that it is the freedom to love and serve the rest of the Christian family.

We must be careful that we don't think of this as the other side of the coin. There is no other side to the coin of freedom! Some have taught that Paul, on the one hand teaches about freedom, and then on the other, the importance of living to the rules, as if it were possible to have too much freedom. This is not the case. We can never have too much freedom, and the Living God is utterly and absolutely free. Instead, Paul simply describes what that Christian freedom looks like in practice and how Christians should use that wonderful freedom. Much like Romans 6, Paul is anxious to point out that as Christians, we are no longer enslaved to sin. Instead, we are free to live the mature lives that God desires for us.

This freedom expresses itself not in selfish individualism, but in the community of the church. Thus this second section of chapter 5 is topped and tailed by references to "each other" (see verses 13, 15 and 26).

Now that his readers know about their freedom, Paul wants to ensure that they use that freedom properly. It is interesting that Paul doesn't just say 'love one another'. That would be too passive. In light of the freedom he has been advocating, he demands an action, the action of **service** done in love. Real love is action and service, never sentiment alone (verse 13).

If the Galatian Christians really wanted to obey the Law, then, says Paul (verse 14), why don't they do what the Law **really** required rather than what the 'circumcision group' taught? The Law taught Israel not only to trust in the Messiah, but to do this with lives full of loving service to their neighbours. The command to serve one another in love is not a new thing from the Messiah. This was what the Law actually said in Leviticus 19:18.

5. Walking in the Spirit, verses 16-26

So what's the alternative to living by the Law? How can Christians live a life that is pleasing to God and that shows love to fellow Christians, if there is no Law to rule our lives?

The answer, says Paul, is simple (verse 16). Live by the reality and not the mere sign. Live by the Spirit. Follow the signpost and go straight to the destination. Recognise that there is a constant battle going on between the flesh and the Spirit, and in your freedom, choose the way of the Spirit, verse 17. If you do choose to live by the Spirit, to let the Spirit lead your thoughts and actions and attitudes, then you will not live the life of the flesh and destroy each other.

To trust in the Spirit of Christ for our daily living is obviously in opposition to trusting in the Law for our daily living. To be led by the Spirit is to be free from the leading of the Law (verse 18).

The way of the Spirit is in complete contrast to the life of the flesh. They are mutually exclusive. The conflict that Paul describes is very real and very difficult.[6] We want to be in full harmony with the Spirit, but our flesh wants to live the very opposite. We often find ourselves doing the very things we hate. We know what we want to do but we do something completely different.

However, the mere fact that we don't want to sin, is a sign of our being born again. We are therefore to take courage in the fight. There is no point in trusting in the Law to overcome the flesh: it is only Christ by His Spirit who can do that.

The sinful nature engages in acts (plural) and these acts are obvious.[7] The list Paul gives is quite a catalogue and seems to address our attitude toward sexuality (sexual immorality, immorality and debauchery); our attitude towards God (idolatry and witchcraft); our attitude towards other people (hatred, discord, jealousy, fits of rage, selfish ambition, dissensions, factions and envy); and our attitude towards ourselves (drunkenness and orgies).

Paul's warning is quite clear. **If a person is enslaved to such a life they have not yet been set free by Jesus**. They are not yet born again and will not inherit the kingdom of God.

The fruit of the Spirit is singular (verses 22–23). Unlike the myriad of acts of the sinful nature (Paul doesn't even give us a complete list but finishes with "and the like"), the life marked out by the Spirit is one life. It is a life marked by one type of lifestyle, not many types.

There is no law that can either stand against such things or bring such things to be. They are the outward workings of the Spirit in a person's life. When a person becomes a new creation (Galatians 6:15, 2 Corinthians 5:17), they are like a new tree bearing new fruit.[8]

---

[6] See also Romans chapter 7

[7] Note the difference between "acts" (plural) and "fruit" (singular) in verse 22.

[8] See also Matthew 7:16-20 and Matthew 12:33-35.

Paul uses a surprising word to describe what has happened to the flesh, verse 24. He describes it as "crucified" – nailed up on the Cross. Luther again: "Although it is still alive, it cannot do what it wants since it is bound hand and foot."[9] **Only those who are born again can know and experience the joy and freedom of being able to say 'no' to evil desires**.

As Christians we do live by the Spirit (verse 25). That is where our life comes from, so Paul finishes here by encouraging his readers to "keep in step with the Spirit" – to keep walking as He walks, following His direction, standing where He stands.

If we are not doing verse 13 – serving one another in love – then we will do verse 15 and 26 – bite and devour each other. Thus to live by the Spirit is the way to serve one another and avoid devouring or provoking each other.

"They (the Galatians) should not strive against one another, verses 13–15. They should strive against sin." Matthew Henry's Commentary.

[9] Luther's commentary on Galatians. Crossways Classic Commentary edition. Page 282.

Further Questions ...

1. In what ways did the Law point to and show the gospel?

2. What is the difference between a Christian who is living a sinful life, and a non-Christian who always does good things?

Daily Readings ...

Day 1:	Galatians chapter 5
Day 2:	Romans chapter 3
Day 3:	Hebrews chapter 12
Day 4:	Psalm 51
Day 5:	Romans chapter 7
Day 6:	1 Peter 2:16–25
Day 7:	1 John 1:5–2:11

Bible Study 5

Chapter 5:13–25

Having explained our total freedom in Christ, Paul goes on to tell us what this freedom means in practical terms.

How had the Galatians been using their freedom? (1:6, 4:9)

In what ways can we use our freedom, verse 13?

The 'circumcision group' amongst the Galatians thought they were keeping the Law by trying to trust in it for salvation. Why were they actually breaking it by what they were doing? Verse 14 & 2:12.

What does sin do to us as Christians? (verses 16–17, see also 1 Peter 2:11)

Why shouldn't we want to sin if we are born again by the Spirit?

In what way is freedom from sin true freedom? (Romans 6:17–18)

Why is how we live our lives so important? Are there any similarities here between the life of the unbeliever (verses 19–21) and the Christian (verse 22–24)? (See 2 Corinthians 6:14–15)

What role does the Holy Spirit have in the unity of the Church and in our growth as Christians?

How can we "keep in step with the Spirit"?, verse 25.

Study 6, Galatians Chapter 6

Brothers, the Family of Believers

Key Truth: Now that Paul has explained the purpose of the Law and the meaning of freedom, he gives us a picture of what this freedom in the Church looks like.

1. Living in the Spirit Together, verses 1–5

Paul continues to show us what true freedom looks like in practice. How should we use our freedom to get the maximum value from it?

Chapter 5:26 is the transition from warning us away from the flesh to showing us what 'walking with the Spirit' looks like. We should not use our freedom to be arrogant, boasting about how we live, or all that we can get away with. If we boast about how 'daring' or how 'worldly' or how 'wealthy' we can be, we show no concern for our fellow Christians. Such behaviour simply creates division, provoking each other to envy.

So, as we get into chapter 6, Paul assumes that we are turning away from the arrogance and conceit of the flesh and turning towards the full enjoyment of our freedom.

Rather than using our freedom to cause each other to sin, we should use our freedom to help each other not to sin (6:1). The mark of the spiritual person is that when they see a fellow Christian struggling with sin and the flesh, they will do all that they can to restore them with a spirit of **gentleness**. We are so gentle in restoring each other because we are acutely aware of how utterly vulnerable we are to our own flesh. It is only the gracious, gentle work of the Spirit that keeps us free from such slavery.

There is something almost witty about verse 2. The Law belongs to the Messiah. It is **Christ's** Law, and fulfilling the Law is all about obeying, trusting and following the Messiah. Like in 5:14, Paul challenges the Galatians to do what the Law was really pointing to, rather than what the 'circumcision group' thought that it was commanding. It is almost as if

Paul was saying, "if you're all fired up for fulfilling the Law, why not do what the Law **really** wants you to do – that is: carry each other's burdens, in love, for the sake of Christ Jesus".

(Verses 4–5) We are actually attacking the real purpose of the Law if we take pride in how much stronger we think we are than others in the Church – taking pride in our own righteousness. We have no righteousness other than that which we have in Christ, and we all have that together, equally as His body. Instead of trying to police each other's discipleship, we should concern ourselves only with the faithfulness of our own hearts.

2. Investing in the Word of God, verses 6–10

In verse 6 Paul commands us to share all the good things we have with our Bible teachers. What does he mean by this? He is telling us to invest all that we have in Bible teaching. The resources that we have been given must be used for the best possible purpose, the teaching of the Word.

What are we going to invest in throughout our lives?

Our heavenly Father, in His great kindness, gives us all kinds of things to use, whether time or money or skills or connections or property or relationships. He has entrusted us with these resources and the great question of life is this: do we store up treasure in heaven or treasure on earth? Do we invest in the future or merely in the present? Do we hoard our resources for our own benefit or do we treat them all as really belonging to the family of God? Do we dream of a nice house in the country, the latest technology, a top education for our children or that beautiful car … or do we dream about the Bible being faithfully, courageously taught in every town in the whole nation? What do we really want from life?

Paul tells us how to order our priorities. The good things we have in life are used best of all when they are invested in the teaching of the Word of God. The teaching of the Word must be the great obsession of every Christian, because it is by the Word of God that lives are transformed as people encounter Jesus Christ in the Bible. When we read Psalm 1 or Psalm 119 we catch the heart beat of Biblical spirituality. It is a love relationship with the Living God through His living and ever-new Word.

Where our treasure is, there our heart is also. The area of life we commit our resources to, that is what we will care about the most. If we make the decision to support the teaching of the Bible in every way that we can, then the teaching of the Bible will be the most important thing in our lives. If we want a fruitful life in the eyes of the Father, Son and Holy Spirit, then we must pursue their agenda, which is the truth of the Bible, lived and explained with grace and love.

There are hundreds of people, charismatically gifted to explain the Bible, who do not have the financial, social and administrative support to spend their lives teaching the Word. If I do not possess the gifts to take the Bible onto the streets or into the local school, then I least I can give the gifts and resources that I **do** have in order to enable other members of the Christian family to do these things. In that way the street evangelism, the school work, the home groups, the weekly Bible teaching, the evangelistic courses, the missionaries and all the ways in which the Bible is taught can become **my ministry** too, whatever other gifts I possess.

Verses 7–9 continue to make us think about using our resources for the teaching of the Word. The way we use our resources in life shows what we **really** believe in, what we **really** value. We might say that we believe in and love Jesus, but the use of our resources tells us the **real** story.

If we want to know what a person's spirituality really is, check out their wallet and their diary. Check their bank balance – what are they investing in? We can say that we love Jesus, but this is the way we can really tell the truth about ourselves: look at our diaries and see what we spend our time doing. Look at our wallets to find out where our money is being spent, what we are prepared to dig deep for. When we see the real state of our wallets and diaries then we discover what we **really** love in life, regardless of what we **say**.

If our lives are invested in this passing life, then the true state of our hearts are obvious, and we will certainly reap the harvest of destruction when Jesus returns (verse 8). If our lives are invested in that future when Jesus returns, showing that we love and trust Him, then we will reap a harvest which will last forever and ever.

Paul's knows how easy it is to be discouraged when we do this. We live in a world and a culture that is focussed on investing in the here and now. So, verse 9, Paul encourages us to keep going towards that wonderful future, even when we are weary and disillusioned. We will definitely not be disappointed by the Living God on the Day of Harvest.

We're waiting for the harvest. The Word of God is the only seed that will actually produce the harvest worth having. This is what Jesus taught in Luke 8:1–21. The Day of Harvest reveals what we have done with the Word of God. That Day will reveal what kind of soil we are – Luke 8:18. If the concerns of this life are what ultimately matter to you more than the Word, the Word will be choked out eventually (Luke 8:7 & 14). The mark of being good soil is that we love the Word and it bubbles over. The family of Jesus are those who hear the Word and share it, do it, speak about it, enthuse about it (Luke 8:21).

In Galatians 6:10 Paul gathers the thought to a conclusion. We don't become weary in doing good (investing in the Word of God). In fact, our lives should be all about finding opportunities to do this good to everybody we meet, especially to the family of believers. We have our eyes on the Day of Harvest and we desperately want everybody we meet to have a harvest of eternal life rather than a harvest of destruction.

3. The New Creation, verses 11–18

In all his letters, Paul would sign them at the end, (see 2 Thessalonians 3:17). However, it looks as if Paul wrote the whole letter of Galatians himself rather than using a 'secretary' as he seemed to do at other times (Romans 16:22, for example).

Paul has made this personal gesture perhaps because of the intensely personal nature of this letter. Paul has bared his soul to the Galatians. He has given us his spiritual biography and allowed us to see what the deep emotions of his heart are all about.

In verse 12 he continues this personal atmosphere. In order to stand against 'the circumcision group' Paul has had to endure a life of persecution and hardship. Standing firm on the total sufficiency of the Cross of the Messiah has forced Paul to be continuously opposed. All those who trusted in the Law hated Paul for his total confidence in Jesus, His death and resurrection. If even the mighty apostle Peter compromised on his gospel lifestyle when faced with persecution from 'the circumcision group', then we can see how much pain must lie behind verse 12 for the apostle Paul.

There is a lesson for us too here. Standing for the truth about Jesus the Messiah will always be costly and will always bring persecution. 2 Timothy 3:12 – "everyone who wants to live a godly life in Christ Jesus will be persecuted ..." The human heart is flesh, as Galatians 5 has made clear to us. Galatians 5:17 warned us that the flesh and the Holy Spirit are at war. This is no vague theory, but a practical reality. If we explain that Jesus is the Messiah, the Son of God, and that the only way of avoiding Hell is by trusting in His death and resurrection, we will certainly face some severe ridicule and opposition sooner or later. Paul encourages us, by his own example, to stand firm and remain faithful to Jesus.

The 'circumcision group' may claim to keep the Law, but, as the whole letter of Galatians has so clearly shown, they do not keep the Law as it was originally intended (verse 13). Their kind of Law-keeping is really Law-breaking because it ignores the Promised Messiah. The sole purpose of the Law was to make people trust in the Promised Seed until He actually arrived. On the basis of 3:24 and 5:14, keeping the Law means trusting in Christ and living in love. Because the circumcisers do neither of these things, in no sense can they be described as keeping the Law.[1]

So, when we finally get everything out into the open, we can see that what they really want to do is boast in the flesh (verse 13), which is the very opposite of the Spirit. Their bragging reveals where their confidence lies, which links neatly into verse 14. Paul is horrified about such bragging. The only bragging that is acceptable to the Living God is the bragging of the Cross ... because **that** bragging is the condemnation and destruction of the flesh. The circumcisers wanted to be able to parade these Gentile converts and get respect and credit from their fellow unbelieving Israelites. What they wanted from life was respect from others who also trusted in the Law. Their glory was completely wrapped up in **this** world with its social structures and accomplishments.

By the cross of Jesus, our natural life in the world is executed, and therefore, all the glory and confidence of this world with all its social approval and earthly respect is denied us (verse 14). But because it is denied us, it holds no power over us. We are set free from the petty and meaningless agendas of the flesh. We do not seek the affirmation of any accept the Father, Son and Holy Spirit. This is why Christians are so often the most radical members of any society or culture.

So whether we are circumcised or not circumcised (verse 15), whether we were born under the system of Law or born in darkest Paganism, it has no meaning whatsoever as to what we really are in Jesus Christ. Through the gospel, all fleshly grounds for boasting or shame are redundant. By trusting in Christ, we become part of the New Creation of the future. What we were in the old creation is irrelevant.

The peace and mercy of God is given to those who live by this rule, verse 16 – the rule that all distinctions between Jew and Gentile are rendered irrelevant by the new birth in Christ. Therefore, Paul concludes with a triumphant assertion of the real meaning of Israel. The Israel of the flesh (1 Corinthians 10:18, see also Romans 9:6) defines itself according to fleshly definitions – where you were born, who your parents were,

---

[1] It is not that the circumcisers sometimes broke the Law because the Law itself accommodates such things and has instructions about what to do when you break it. Some people say that if a person under the Law committed a single sin, they had failed the way of salvation offered by the Law. In fact, a large part of the Law is dealing with infringements of the Law! The majority of the Law, from the construction and function of the Tabernacle to the sacrificial system, is all dealing with people under the Law **breaking the Law**. Thus, the Law was designed to govern sinners and point them to the coming Messiah, the Lamb of God, for salvation. A sinner who trusted in the coming Messiah was the true Law-keeper.

whether you are circumcised or not. But this has nothing to do with the Israel of God, either in the Old Testament or the New Testament. The Israel of God is defined as the new creation in Christ where all worldly definitions are meaningless.

So in verse 16, Paul says that **the peace and mercy that belong to Israel really belong to all those whether Jew or Gentile who live by the gospel of Jesus Christ**.

Paul concludes his letter, and there is something of a weariness about the great apostle after the titanic struggle of this letter against the false gospel. He wants no more trouble (verse 17) because his life has been a life of suffering trouble for the sake of Christ. His very body testifies to how he has steadfastly endured the persecution that preaching the cross of Christ inevitably brings. 2 Corinthians 11:23–28 is a catalogue of the scars and injuries that he refers to here. With that, Paul gives us his typical ending (see Philemon 25 and 2 Timothy 4:22) wishing only that the friendship and love of Jesus Christ be our all in all.

Further Questions ...

1. People often quote verse 7, "do not be deceived: God cannot be mocked" as a phrase by itself. But what does Paul really mean here?

2. Some people use 6:10 to promote Christian involvement in general humanitarian work. Why is that an incorrect use of this verse here?

Daily Readings ...

Day 1:	Galatians chapter 6
Day 2:	1 Corinthians chapter 8
Day 3:	Luke 8:1–21
Day 4:	Psalm 1 & Psalm 119:97–104
Day 5:	1 Corinthians 10:23–11:1
Day 6:	1 Peter chapter 4
Day 7:	Matthew 6:19–24 & 11:25–29

Bible Study 6

Chapter 5:26–6:10

What are the characteristics of Christians understanding and living in the freedom that the gospel brings? Paul concludes his letter with some practical help.

How does 5:26 link chapter 6 with the teaching on the Spirit to chapter 5? Doesn't it seem like an odd verse with which to begin a study?

Why is 6:1 a important thing to note when talking about Christian freedom? (See 1 Corinthians 10:32–33)

Don't verses 2 & 5 seem to be saying opposite things? How can we explain these verses? What is the difference between 'burden', verse 2 and 'load', verse 5?

Verses 6–10 talk about investing in Bible teaching. Why are we told to do this, especially in the context of the whole church united together?

In what ways do verses 7–8 challenge us to examine our lives and the use of our time and resources?

How can we live as Christians ensuring we are pleasing the Spirit?

How is it possible to persevere in these things, verses 9 & 10? How can we encourage one another to keep living for the LORD and investing in Bible teaching?

What are the key things you have learnt from our studies on the book of Galatians that will help you in your relationship with the LORD, and also with other believers.